THE
SPECTATOR
CARTOON BOOK
2000

Edited by
Michael Heath

PROFILE BOOKS
in association with
The Spectator

First published
in book form in Great Britain in 2000 by
Profile Books Ltd
58A Hatton Garden, London EC1N 8LX
in association with
The Spectator
56 Doughty Street, London WC1N 2LL

© The Spectator, 2000

Typeset by MacGuru
info@macguru.org.uk

Printed and bound in Great Britain by
St Edmundsbury Press Ltd

A CIP catalogue record for this book is available from
the British Library.

ISBN 1 86197 248 2

"I keep putting up barriers."

"Thank heavens! This year it's OK not to slavishly follow the dictates of popular fashion."

DUNLYNCHIN

"That last mint … I told you it was mine."

"The Sixties? Well, you don't sleep as well, can't read anything closer than three feet away, and your short-term memory's shot."

"Who taught her to beg?"

"Oh, I can't sing. I can only eat like him."

"Sometimes I feel like running off and closing down a circus."

"Now they'll all have to be grounded."

"Already my boy's a babe-magnet."

SIPRESS

*"Hold everything! I can't sleep with you —
these aren't 100 per cent cotton."*

"An after-sex cigarette just isn't the same
in a no-smoking house."

"You think you're invisible.
Try being a middle-aged woman!"

"I just think we'd be a better fighting unit
if it didn't take us two hours to get dressed."

"Hi, it's me. I'm on the terrine!"

"There was an Englishman, an Irishman and a Scotsman …"

"Where, may I ask, is your advertised ambience?"

"Every day he returns Groundhog Day,
only to rent it out again."

"Hello, Nasa, how much would it cost to put a rocket up my teenage son's backside?"

"'Ere, this is nuffink like opium."

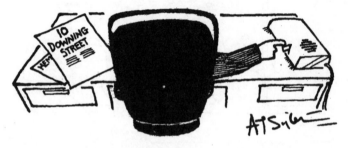

"Take a leak!"

"Trouble at website, lass."

"That was a metaphorical call to gird up our loins, Miss Thring."

"Just once I'd like to be mad, bad and dangerous to know."

"We were on our way home from the park
when all of a sudden he ran away."

"I can *make a reservation for tonight*? Then clearly yours is
not the kind of restaurant we wish to be seen in."

"We've had 60 billion applications."

"Those are my parents shouting at each other."

"Say, Dad — this story is the same as last night's story."

"This is a lot more satisfying than those dinky old circus horns."

*"I really don't mind where we visit next.
To me, one place is very much like another."*

"Something for the weekend, sir?"

First gay airline

*"I'm going to walk around the school —
keep me under constant surveillance."*

"If you want people to trust you and your message, shave off your beard."

"I like you, you've got balls."

"I got this one for stress!"

*"Forget it, Nigel, you'll look ridiculous —
everyone knows you're a grey squirrel."*

"He talks to himself."

"Oh look, darling, his first outmoded technology."

"Aren't you due for a check-up, George?"

"Come in for a chat, I'm a Jehovah's Witness."

"Excuse me, madam, I couldn't help noticing that you were driving erotically."

"Off you go to school. Here's your protection money."

*"We look utterly ridiculous!
These dresses went out in the Seventies."*

"Try it a bit lower."

*"You've seen his cubist period —
this is his giving-up-smoking period."*

"Oh, yeah? Well my nanny makes forty thousand a year."

"But that's what chimps of today do at parties — get drunk, take drugs, have sex and throw up everywhere."

"What do you mean, we have to go to church today?"

"Did you know that in Hampstead
they have 50 different names for bread?"

ROBERT THOMPSON

"Do you have any diet water?"

"It's not the murder weapon, sir, but it could be the motive."

"… Tall, dark hair, big blue eyes, and long legs all the way up to my neck …"

*"You're invited to some sort of jamboree —
you're expected to donate a kidney."*

"Forget the flowers, Vincent, just exhibit the bed."

"Single mums are so passé my dear, what you need is a double mum."

"You wear pyjamas!"

"Shall I dish the dirt, ladies?"

OOH, I LIKE WHAT YOU'RE WEARING
THANKS, IT'S TOMATO SAUCE
ROBERT THOMPSON

"Be careful, son, it's like a housing estate out there."

"Germans."

"No, he doesn't want an apple."

"As far as I'm concerned, no muse is good muse."

*"Couldn't you let your speech-writer knock off
a little light conversation?"*

*"I'm the man in the iron mask and
this is the man in the ironic mask."*